Mastering LinkedIn Marketing

Unlocking the Power of Professional Networking

Alex Westwood

Copyright © [Year] by Alex Westwood

All rights reserved. No part of this book may be reproduced, distributed, or transmitted in any form or by any means, including photocopying, recording, or other electronic or mechanical methods, without the prior written permission of the author, except in the case of brief quotations embodied in critical reviews and certain other noncommercial uses permitted by copyright law.

TABLE OF CONTENT

Introduction **5**
Chapter 1 10
   Optimizing Your LinkedIn Profile **10**
Chapter 2 17
   Building a Strong LinkedIn Network **17**
Chapter 3 23
   Creating Compelling Content on LinkedIn **23**
Chapter 4 29
   Leveraging LinkedIn Company Pages **29**
Chapter 5 35
   Using LinkedIn for Thought Leadership **35**
Chapter 6 40
   Maximizing Lead Generation on LinkedIn **40**
Chapter 7 45
   Nurturing Relationships and Building Trust **45**
Chapter 8 52
   Measuring Success with LinkedIn Analytics **52**
Chapter 9 58
   LinkedIn Recruiting and Talent Acquisition **58**
Chapter 10 64
   International and Global LinkedIn Marketing **64**
Chapter 11 69
   Future Trends in LinkedIn Marketing **69**
Appendix 76

Tools for LinkedIn Marketing 76

Conclusion 81

    Unleashing the Full Potential of LinkedIn for Your Business or Professional Career 81

Introduction

Welcome to the world of LinkedIn marketing! In this book, we will explore the vast opportunities and potential that LinkedIn offers as a powerful marketing platform. As one of the largest professional social networking sites, LinkedIn provides a unique space for businesses and professionals to connect, network, and promote their products and services.

LinkedIn has grown exponentially since its inception in 2003, boasting over 774 million members in more than 200 countries and territories. It has become the go-to platform for professionals looking to expand their network, showcase their expertise, and discover new career opportunities. However, LinkedIn is not just a platform for individuals—it also serves as a valuable marketing tool for businesses of all sizes.

Understanding the potential of LinkedIn as a marketing platform is crucial in today's digital landscape. With its extensive user base, LinkedIn provides access to a highly targeted and engaged audience. Whether you are a small business owner, a marketer, a freelancer, or a professional seeking to build your personal brand,

LinkedIn offers a plethora of features and tools to help you achieve your marketing goals.

The importance of LinkedIn for businesses and professionals cannot be overstated. It has transformed the way people connect and do business, bridging the gap between professionals across industries and geographies. LinkedIn allows businesses to establish their brand, connect with potential clients and partners, recruit top talent, and generate leads and conversions. Professionals can use LinkedIn to showcase their skills, network with like-minded individuals, gain industry insights, and stay updated with the latest trends.

In this book, we will delve into various aspects of LinkedIn marketing and provide you with a comprehensive guide to help you master this platform. From optimizing your profile and building a strong network to creating compelling content and utilizing LinkedIn's advertising features, we will explore proven strategies and best practices that will elevate your LinkedIn marketing efforts.

We will discuss the importance of crafting a compelling personal or company profile that captures attention and resonates with your target audience. We will explore how to build a strong network of connections, foster meaningful relationships, and engage with LinkedIn groups to expand your reach and influence.

Content creation is a key aspect of LinkedIn marketing, and we will provide insights on creating engaging articles, posts, and videos that captivate your audience and establish your thought leadership. Additionally, we will dive into the world of LinkedIn advertising, showcasing how you can leverage sponsored content and targeted ads to reach your ideal customers and drive conversions.

Measuring success is vital in any marketing strategy, and we will explore how to use LinkedIn's analytics tools to track your performance, identify areas of improvement, and optimize your marketing campaigns for better results.

Furthermore, we will discuss the role of LinkedIn in talent acquisition and recruitment, providing valuable tips and strategies to attract top talent and build a strong employer brand. We will also explore international LinkedIn marketing, helping you expand your reach and connect with a global audience.

Finally, we will look towards the future of LinkedIn marketing and discuss emerging trends and features that will shape the platform's evolution. Staying ahead in the dynamic world of LinkedIn marketing requires adaptability and an understanding of the changing user behaviors and platform updates.

By the end of this book, you will have a comprehensive understanding of LinkedIn marketing and the tools and strategies needed to succeed. Whether you are a business owner, marketer, freelancer, or professional, this book will equip you with the knowledge and skills to leverage LinkedIn's potential for growth, visibility, and professional success.

So, let's embark on this LinkedIn marketing journey together and unlock the power of professional networking to elevate your personal brand or business to new heights.

Chapter 1

Optimizing Your LinkedIn Profile

In the world of LinkedIn marketing, your profile serves as the cornerstone of your online presence. It is your digital representation and the first impression you make on potential connections, clients, and employers. Optimizing your LinkedIn profile is crucial to ensure that you stand out from the crowd and attract the right opportunities. In this chapter, we will explore the essential elements of crafting an impressive LinkedIn profile and optimizing it for maximum visibility and searchability.

1.1 Crafting an Impressive LinkedIn Profile

Your LinkedIn profile is more than just an online resume. It is an opportunity to showcase your expertise, highlight your achievements, and tell your professional story. To craft an impressive LinkedIn profile, consider the following elements:

1.1.1 Professional Headline: Your professional headline appears beneath your name and should effectively summarize your expertise and value proposition. Use keywords relevant to your industry to make it easily discoverable in search results.

1.1.2 Profile Photo: Choose a professional and high-quality profile photo that represents your personal brand. A friendly and approachable headshot will help build trust and credibility.

1.1.3 Background Photo: The background photo is a valuable visual space that allows you to express your personality and showcase your professional interests. Use an image that aligns with your industry or personal brand.

1.1.4 Summary: Your LinkedIn summary is an opportunity to tell your story, highlight your unique selling points, and convey your professional goals. Craft a compelling summary that engages the reader and showcases your expertise and achievements.

1.1.5 Experience and Education: Provide detailed information about your work experience and educational background. Highlight your key responsibilities, accomplishments, and notable projects. Use bullet points and concise language to make it easy to read and understand.

1.1.6 Skills and Endorsements: List relevant skills that showcase your expertise. Encourage colleagues and connections to endorse your skills to boost credibility.

1.1.7 Recommendations: Request recommendations from colleagues, clients, or supervisors who can vouch for your skills and work ethic. Positive recommendations can enhance your professional reputation.

1.1.8 Accomplishments: Utilize the "Accomplishments" section to showcase awards, certifications, publications, volunteer work, or any other noteworthy achievements. This section adds depth to your profile and demonstrates your commitment to professional development.

1.1.9 Contact Information: Ensure that your contact information, including your email address and website, is up to date. Make it easy for interested parties to reach out to you.

1.2 Highlighting Your Expertise and Professional Achievements

LinkedIn is a platform designed to showcase your expertise and professional achievements. To make your profile stand out, consider the following strategies:

1.2.1 Keywords: Incorporate relevant keywords throughout your profile to increase search visibility. Research industry-specific terms and phrases to ensure your profile aligns with the language used in your field.

1.2.2 Showcasing Achievements: Highlight your accomplishments, awards, and certifications in the "Experience" and "Accomplishments" sections. Quantify your achievements whenever possible to provide concrete evidence of your success.

1.2.3 Multimedia Content: Utilize LinkedIn's multimedia features to enhance your profile. Include relevant images, videos, presentations, or documents that showcase your work or provide additional context to your expertise.

1.2.4 Publications and Posts: Share your thought leadership by publishing articles or posts on LinkedIn. This demonstrates your industry knowledge and can attract attention from peers and potential clients.

1.2.5 Volunteer Experience: If applicable, include your volunteer experience to showcase your commitment to social causes and community involvement. It can reflect positively on your personal brand and values.

1.3 Optimizing Your Profile for LinkedIn Search

LinkedIn's search algorithm plays a crucial role in connecting professionals with relevant opportunities. To optimize your profile for LinkedIn search, consider the following strategies:

1.3.1 Keyword Research: Conduct keyword research to identify the terms and phrases commonly used in your industry. Incorporate these keywords strategically throughout your profile, including your headline, summary, and experience sections.

1.3.2 Complete Your Profile: LinkedIn rewards users with complete profiles by ranking them higher in search results. Ensure that you fill out all sections of your profile, including education, certifications, and volunteer experience.

1.3.3 Build Connections: Growing your network increases your visibility on LinkedIn. Connect with professionals in your industry, join relevant groups, and engage in meaningful conversations to expand your reach.

1.3.4 Engage with Content: Actively engage with posts and articles in your feed. Liking, commenting, and sharing relevant content can increase your visibility and attract the attention of other professionals in your field.

1.3.5 Regular Updates: Keep your profile up to date with your latest accomplishments, projects, and skills. Regularly update your profile to reflect your current professional status.

By optimizing your LinkedIn profile, highlighting your expertise, and making it search-friendly, you significantly increase your chances of attracting the right connections, clients, and opportunities. Take the time to craft a compelling and comprehensive profile that effectively communicates your professional brand and sets you apart in the competitive world of LinkedIn marketing.

Chapter 2

Building a Strong LinkedIn Network

In the realm of LinkedIn marketing, building a strong network is key to expanding your reach, establishing valuable connections, and nurturing meaningful relationships with professionals in your industry. In this chapter, we will explore effective strategies for expanding your connections, leveraging LinkedIn Groups for networking and engagement, and using LinkedIn Events to connect with industry professionals.

2.1 Expanding Your Connections and Building Meaningful Relationships

Expanding your LinkedIn network goes beyond simply collecting connections. It involves cultivating meaningful relationships with professionals who can provide value, support, and opportunities. Consider the following strategies to build a strong LinkedIn network:

2.1.1 Define Your Target Audience: Determine the types of professionals you want to connect with on LinkedIn.

Identify individuals who align with your industry, interests, and professional goals.

2.1.2 Personalize Connection Requests: When sending connection requests, personalize your messages to demonstrate genuine interest and relevance. Explain why you want to connect and how you can potentially add value to each other.

2.1.3 Engage with Content: Actively engage with posts, articles, and updates shared by your connections. Like, comment, and share valuable content to establish yourself as an engaged and knowledgeable professional.

2.1.4 Attend Networking Events: Look for networking events, both online and offline, related to your industry. Attend conferences, webinars, and seminars to meet professionals face-to-face and establish meaningful connections.

2.1.5 Request Introductions: Utilize your existing connections to request introductions to individuals you would like to connect with. A warm introduction increases the likelihood of establishing a valuable relationship.

2.1.6 Provide Value: Offer help, insights, and support to your connections whenever possible. Share relevant resources, provide recommendations, and offer your expertise to build trust and credibility.

2.1.7 Maintain Relationships: Regularly engage with your connections by congratulating them on their achievements, acknowledging their work, and reaching out for meaningful conversations. Nurture your relationships to ensure they remain strong and mutually beneficial.

2.2 Leveraging LinkedIn Groups for Networking and Engagement

LinkedIn Groups provide an excellent platform for networking, engaging with professionals in your industry, and showcasing your expertise. To effectively leverage LinkedIn Groups, consider the following strategies:

2.2.1 Join Relevant Groups: Identify and join LinkedIn Groups that align with your industry, interests, and professional goals. Look for groups with active discussions and engaged members.

2.2.2 Engage in Conversations: Actively participate in group discussions by sharing valuable insights, asking questions, and contributing to meaningful conversations. Establish yourself as a knowledgeable and helpful professional.

2.2.3 Provide Value: Share relevant articles, resources, and tips with the group to position yourself as a thought leader. Provide insights and solutions to challenges faced by group members.

2.2.4 Network with Group Members: Take the opportunity to connect with individuals who contribute valuable insights or share similar interests. Send personalized connection requests to foster deeper relationships.

2.2.5 Start Meaningful Discussions: Initiate discussions on topics of interest within the group. Pose thought-provoking questions and encourage members to share their insights and experiences.

2.2.6 Respect Group Rules and Guidelines: Familiarize yourself with the group's rules and guidelines and abide by them. Ensure your contributions are relevant, respectful, and add value to the group's discussions.

2.3 Using LinkedIn Events to Connect with Industry Professionals

LinkedIn Events provide a powerful platform for connecting with industry professionals, promoting your brand, and organizing virtual or in-person gatherings. Consider the following strategies to leverage LinkedIn Events effectively:

2.3.1 Organize Events: Host virtual or in-person events on LinkedIn to showcase your expertise, promote your brand, or facilitate networking opportunities.

Choose event formats that resonate with your target audience.

2.3.2 Promote Your Events: Utilize LinkedIn's event promotion tools to raise awareness and attract attendees. Leverage your network, LinkedIn Groups, and other social media channels to spread the word about your event.

2.3.3 Engage with Attendees: Actively engage with attendees before, during, and after the event. Respond to comments, address questions, and follow up with participants to foster relationships.

2.3.4 Collaborate with Others: Consider partnering with industry influencers, organizations, or professionals to co-host events. Collaborative events can expand your reach and attract a diverse audience.

2.3.5 Follow Up after Events: Send personalized messages to event attendees to thank them for their participation and to continue building relationships. Share relevant resources or insights discussed during the event.

Building a strong LinkedIn network requires a proactive and strategic approach. By expanding your connections, engaging with professionals through LinkedIn Groups, and utilizing LinkedIn Events, you can establish a robust network of valuable connections. Remember to prioritize quality over quantity and nurture your relationships for long-term success in your LinkedIn marketing endeavors.

Chapter 3

Creating Compelling Content on LinkedIn

In the realm of LinkedIn marketing, creating compelling content is essential to capture the attention of your audience, establish your expertise, and drive engagement. This chapter will explore the types of content that perform well on LinkedIn, provide insights into crafting engaging articles and posts, and discuss the benefits of leveraging LinkedIn's native video feature.

3.1 Understanding the Types of Content That Perform Well on LinkedIn

To create compelling content on LinkedIn, it's crucial to understand the types of content that resonate with your audience and drive engagement. While every audience is unique, certain content formats tend to perform well on LinkedIn. Consider the following types of content:

3.1.1 Thought Leadership Articles: LinkedIn provides an excellent platform for sharing in-depth, thought-provoking articles that showcase your expertise. These articles should provide valuable insights, industry trends, and actionable advice for your audience.

3.1.2 Industry News and Updates: Sharing timely and relevant industry news helps position you as a knowledgeable professional. Stay updated with the latest trends, developments, and news in your industry and provide commentary or insights to spark conversations.

3.1.3 Case Studies and Success Stories: Share success stories and case studies that highlight how your products, services, or expertise have helped clients or customers. These stories demonstrate the value you bring and establish trust with your audience.

3.1.4 Infographics and Visual Content: Visual content, such as infographics, charts, and images, can effectively convey complex information in a visually appealing way. Use visuals to enhance your content and capture attention as users scroll through their feeds.

3.1.5 Inspirational and Motivational Posts: LinkedIn users appreciate uplifting and motivational content. Share inspiring stories, quotes, or personal experiences that resonate with your audience and encourage them to pursue their goals.

3.1.6 Videos and Webinars: Videos are highly engaging and can convey information in a more dynamic and personal way. Consider creating informative videos, interviews, or hosting webinars to share valuable insights with your audience.

3.2 Crafting Engaging Articles and Posts

Crafting engaging articles and posts on LinkedIn requires a thoughtful approach. Follow these tips to create content that captures attention and encourages interaction:

3.2.1 Understand Your Audience: Gain insights into your target audience's preferences, challenges, and interests. Tailor your content to address their needs and provide value.

3.2.2 Use Compelling Headlines: Create attention-grabbing headlines that pique curiosity and encourage users to click and read your content. Keep them concise, clear, and compelling.

3.2.3 Provide Value and Insights: Your content should provide unique perspectives, actionable advice, and valuable insights. Offer solutions to common challenges, share success stories, and provide practical tips.

3.2.4 Tell Stories: Humans are wired to connect with stories. Incorporate storytelling elements into your content to make it relatable and engaging. Use anecdotes, personal experiences, or client stories to captivate your audience.

3.2.5 Keep it Concise: LinkedIn users often prefer concise and easily digestible content. Break down complex ideas into bite-sized chunks and use bullet points or subheadings to enhance readability.

3.2.6 Include Call-to-Actions (CTAs): Encourage users to engage with your content by including clear CTAs. Prompt them to comment, share, or engage in discussions to foster interaction.

3.3 Leveraging LinkedIn's Native Video Feature

LinkedIn's native video feature provides a powerful opportunity to connect with your audience in a more dynamic and engaging way. Consider the following benefits and strategies for leveraging LinkedIn's native video feature:

3.3.1 Increased Visibility: Native videos on LinkedIn tend to receive higher visibility and engagement compared to shared links or text-based updates. Take advantage of this feature to reach a wider audience.

3.3.2 Authenticity and Personal Connection: Video allows you to showcase your personality and establish a deeper connection with your audience. Be authentic, share your expertise, and deliver valuable insights through video content.

3.3.3 Educational Content: Use video to educate your audience on industry topics, trends, or tips. Create tutorial videos, how-to guides, or share your expertise through educational content.

3.3.4 Behind-the-Scenes Insights: Provide a glimpse into your work environment, projects, or events through video. Humanize your brand and foster a sense of transparency and authenticity.

3.3.5 Video Interviews and Q&A Sessions: Conduct interviews or host Q&A sessions with industry experts or thought leaders. These videos can attract attention and provide valuable insights for your audience.

3.3.6 Optimizing Video Content: Pay attention to video quality, length, and captions. Keep your videos concise and engaging, add subtitles for accessibility, and optimize for mobile viewing.

Creating compelling content on LinkedIn is a vital aspect of mastering LinkedIn marketing. By understanding the types of content that perform well, crafting engaging articles and posts, and leveraging LinkedIn's native video feature, you can effectively capture the attention of your audience, establish your expertise, and drive meaningful engagement on the platform.

Chapter 4

Leveraging LinkedIn Company Pages

LinkedIn Company Pages serve as a valuable tool for businesses to showcase their brand, engage with their audience, and establish a strong online presence. In this chapter, we will explore the process of setting up and optimizing your LinkedIn Company Page, discuss strategies for showcasing your brand and company culture, and provide insights on engaging your audience with company updates and content.

4.1 Setting Up and Optimizing Your Company Page

Creating a compelling and professional LinkedIn Company Page is the first step toward leveraging the platform to its fullest potential. Follow these guidelines to set up and optimize your Company Page:

4.1.1 Completing the Basic Information: Provide accurate and detailed information about your company, including the company name, logo, description, location, and contact details. Ensure that the information is up to date and consistent with your brand identity.

4.1.2 Customizing the Vanity URL: Customize your Company Page's URL to reflect your brand and make it easier for users to find and remember.

4.1.3 Adding a Banner Image: Choose a visually appealing banner image that represents your brand and captures the attention of visitors to your Company Page. Ensure that the image is high-quality and aligned with your brand identity.

4.1.4 Crafting an Engaging Company Description: Write a compelling and concise company description that highlights your unique value proposition, key offerings, and what sets your company apart from competitors. Use keywords relevant to your industry to optimize the discoverability of your Company Page.

4.1.5 Showcasing Products and Services: Utilize the Products and Services section to highlight your offerings, provide detailed descriptions, and include visuals that showcase your products or services.

4.1.6 Enabling Featured Updates: Feature important updates, announcements, or promotions on your Company Page to increase their visibility and engagement.

4.2 Showcasing Your Brand and Company Culture

Your LinkedIn Company Page offers an excellent platform to showcase your brand identity and company culture. Here are some strategies to effectively showcase your brand:

4.2.1 Consistent Branding: Ensure that your Company Page design, imagery, and tone of voice are consistent with your overall brand identity. Use consistent colors, fonts, and visual elements to create a cohesive and recognizable brand presence.

4.2.2 Visual Storytelling: Use high-quality images, videos, and graphics to tell your brand's story visually. Showcase your office space, employees, events, or product demonstrations to give visitors an inside look at your company culture.

4.2.3 Employee Spotlight: Feature employees on your Company Page to highlight their expertise, accomplishments, and contributions to your organization. This humanizes your brand and fosters a sense of trust and authenticity.

4.2.4 Company Values and Mission: Clearly articulate your company's values, mission, and vision on your Company Page. Demonstrate how your organization is making a positive impact and aligning with your audience's values.

4.3 Engaging Your Audience with Company Updates and Content

Engaging your audience is crucial to building a strong LinkedIn community. Consider the following strategies to effectively engage your audience with company updates and content:

4.3.1 Sharing Relevant and Valuable Content: Share industry news, insights, and thought leadership content that is relevant to your audience. Provide valuable information, tips, and advice that can help them solve challenges or stay updated on industry trends.

4.3.2 Employee-Generated Content: Encourage employees to share company updates, industry-related articles, or their own professional insights. This fosters employee advocacy and extends the reach of your content to their networks.

4.3.3 Engaging Visual Content: Use visuals, such as images, videos, and infographics, to make your updates more engaging and visually appealing. Visual content tends to attract more attention and encourages sharing.

4.3.4 Regular Updates: Consistency is key when it comes to engaging your audience. Post regular updates to keep your Company Page active and stay on top of your audience's feeds. Consider scheduling posts in advance to maintain a consistent posting schedule.

4.3.5 Encouraging Audience Interaction: Prompt your audience to engage with your content by asking questions, seeking opinions, or encouraging them to share their own experiences. Respond to comments and messages promptly to foster two-way communication.

By setting up and optimizing your LinkedIn Company Page, showcasing your brand and company culture, and engaging your audience with relevant updates and content, you can establish a strong presence on LinkedIn, build meaningful connections, and drive valuable engagement.

Chapter 5

Using LinkedIn for Thought Leadership

In today's competitive business landscape, establishing yourself as an industry expert and thought leader is essential for gaining credibility and attracting opportunities. LinkedIn provides an ideal platform for showcasing your expertise, sharing insights, and engaging in meaningful industry conversations. In this chapter, we will explore strategies for using LinkedIn to position yourself as a thought leader, leverage LinkedIn Publishing to share your knowledge, and actively engage in industry conversations through LinkedIn Groups.

5.1 Establishing Yourself as an Industry Expert on LinkedIn

Becoming a recognized industry expert on LinkedIn requires a strategic approach and consistent effort. Consider the following strategies to establish yourself as a thought leader:

5.1.1 Define Your Niche: Identify a specific niche or area of expertise within your industry. Focusing on a niche allows you to differentiate yourself and position yourself as an authority in that particular field.

5.1.2 Optimize Your Profile: Craft a compelling LinkedIn profile that highlights your professional experience, accomplishments, and areas of expertise. Use relevant keywords to optimize your profile for search and clearly communicate your unique value proposition.

5.1.3 Build a Strong Network: Connect with industry professionals, influencers, and peers on LinkedIn. Engage with their content, share valuable insights, and actively participate in conversations within your network.

5.1.4 Share Original Insights: Regularly share your original insights, ideas, and perspectives on industry-related topics. Provide valuable content that educates, informs, and inspires your audience.

5.2 Sharing Insights and Knowledge through LinkedIn Publishing

LinkedIn Publishing is a powerful tool that allows you to share long-form content with your professional network. Here are some tips for leveraging LinkedIn Publishing effectively:

5.2.1 Identify Relevant Topics: Research industry trends, challenges, or emerging topics that are of interest to your target audience. Identify gaps in existing content and focus on providing unique insights and perspectives.

5.2.2 Craft Compelling Articles: Write well-researched, engaging, and informative articles that provide actionable advice, share case studies, or offer thought-provoking insights. Use headings, bullet points, and visuals to make your content more scannable and engaging.

5.2.3 Promote Your Articles: Share your published articles on your LinkedIn feed, relevant LinkedIn Groups, and other social media platforms to increase their visibility. Encourage your network to engage with your content by asking for their opinions or inviting them to share their experiences.

5.2.4 Engage with Comments: Respond to comments on your articles and engage in conversations with your readers. This demonstrates your willingness to interact with your audience and fosters a sense of community.

5.3 Engaging in Industry Conversations and Participating in LinkedIn Groups

LinkedIn Groups provide a valuable opportunity to engage in industry conversations, connect with like-minded professionals, and expand your network. Here's how you can make the most of LinkedIn Groups:

5.3.1 Join Relevant Groups: Identify and join LinkedIn Groups that align with your industry, interests, and target audience. Look for active groups with engaged members and valuable discussions.

5.3.2 Contribute Meaningful Insights: Participate in group discussions by sharing your insights, answering questions, and offering valuable advice. Be respectful and professional in your interactions, and avoid self-promotion or spamming.

5.3.3 Start Thought-Provoking Discussions: Initiate conversations in LinkedIn Groups by posing thought-provoking questions or sharing industry news and insights.

Encourage group members to share their perspectives and engage in meaningful conversations.

5.3.4 Network with Group Members: Connect with active and engaged group members who share similar interests or expertise. Engage with their content, offer support, and build relationships that can lead to collaborations or business opportunities.

By positioning yourself as an industry expert, sharing valuable insights through LinkedIn Publishing, and actively participating in industry conversations and LinkedIn Groups, you can establish yourself as a thought leader on LinkedIn. This not only enhances your professional reputation but also opens doors to new connections, collaborations, and business opportunities.

Chapter 6

Maximizing Lead Generation on LinkedIn

LinkedIn is not only a powerful networking platform but also a valuable tool for generating high-quality leads for your business. In this chapter, we will explore strategies for maximizing lead generation on LinkedIn, including utilizing LinkedIn's lead generation forms and sponsored content, creating effective LinkedIn ad campaigns, and converting LinkedIn connections into qualified leads.

6.1 Utilizing LinkedIn's Lead Generation Forms and Sponsored Content

LinkedIn offers a variety of tools and features specifically designed to capture leads and drive conversions. Here's how you can leverage them effectively:

6.1.1 Understanding LinkedIn's Lead Generation Forms: LinkedIn's lead generation forms simplify the lead capture process by pre-filling contact information from a user's LinkedIn profile. Learn how to set up and customize lead generation forms to collect the most relevant and valuable information from your prospects.

6.1.2 Designing Compelling Sponsored Content: Sponsored content allows you to promote your offers, whitepapers, case studies, or other valuable content to a targeted audience on LinkedIn. Create compelling and visually appealing sponsored content that resonates with your target audience and encourages them to engage and submit their information.

6.1.3 Optimizing Landing Pages: When users click on your sponsored content, they are directed to a landing page. Optimize your landing pages by aligning the messaging and design with your sponsored content, providing clear and concise value propositions, and incorporating strong call-to-action buttons to encourage lead conversions.

6.1.4 Testing and Optimization: Continuously test different variations of your lead generation forms, sponsored content, and landing pages to identify what resonates best with your audience. Use A/B testing to optimize your campaigns and improve conversion rates over time.

6.2 Creating Effective LinkedIn Ad Campaigns

LinkedIn offers various advertising options to help you reach your target audience and generate leads. Consider the following strategies when creating LinkedIn ad campaigns:

6.2.1 Defining Your Campaign Objectives: Clearly define your campaign objectives, whether it's lead generation, brand awareness, or driving website traffic. This will guide your ad creative, targeting, and messaging.

6.2.2 Targeting the Right Audience: Take advantage of LinkedIn's robust targeting options to reach the most relevant audience for your business. Consider factors such as job title, industry, company size, and location to ensure your ads are seen by the right people.

6.2.3 Crafting Compelling Ad Creative: Create visually appealing ad creative that grabs attention and communicates your value proposition clearly. Use compelling headlines, engaging images or videos, and persuasive ad copy to entice users to take action.

6.2.4 Monitoring and Optimization: Monitor the performance of your LinkedIn ad campaigns closely. Analyze metrics such as click-through rates, conversion rates, and cost per lead. Make data-driven decisions to optimize your campaigns and improve their effectiveness.

6.3 Converting LinkedIn Connections into Qualified Leads

Your existing LinkedIn connections can be a valuable source of leads if nurtured and engaged effectively. Consider the following strategies to convert your LinkedIn connections into qualified leads:

6.3.1 Personalized Messaging: Instead of sending generic connection requests or messages, personalize your outreach. Reference a shared interest or connection, and clearly communicate the value you can provide to the recipient.

6.3.2 Building Relationships: Engage with your connections by liking, commenting, and sharing their content. Offer support, share valuable insights, and establish yourself as a helpful and knowledgeable resource.

6.3.3 Offering Value: Provide valuable content, resources, or offers to your connections. This could be in the form of exclusive content, free downloads, or invitations to webinars or events. By offering value, you can build trust and increase the likelihood of them becoming qualified leads.

6.3.4 Tracking and Nurturing

Leads: Use LinkedIn's built-in tools or external customer relationship management (CRM) systems to track and manage your leads. Implement lead nurturing strategies such as automated email campaigns or personalized follow-ups to further engage and convert your connections into customers.

By effectively utilizing LinkedIn's lead generation forms, sponsored content, LinkedIn ad campaigns, and leveraging your existing connections, you can maximize lead generation on LinkedIn. These strategies will help you capture high-quality leads, nurture relationships, and drive meaningful conversions for your business.

Chapter 7

Nurturing Relationships and Building Trust

In the world of business, relationships and trust play a crucial role in building long-term success. On LinkedIn, nurturing relationships and building trust are essential for expanding your network, generating leads, and fostering meaningful connections. In this chapter, we will explore strategies for nurturing relationships and building trust on LinkedIn, including building long-term relationships with LinkedIn connections, providing value through personalized messaging and engagement, and utilizing LinkedIn's Sales Navigator for effective relationship management.

7.1 Building Long-Term Relationships with LinkedIn Connections

While it's important to grow your network on LinkedIn, it's equally important to nurture the relationships you establish. Here are some strategies to help you build long-term relationships with your LinkedIn connections:

7.1.1 Regular Engagement: Engage with your connections regularly by liking, commenting, and sharing their content. Show genuine interest in their updates, offer support, and provide valuable insights. Consistent engagement helps to strengthen relationships and keep you top-of-mind.

7.1.2 Personalized Outreach: When reaching out to new connections or reconnecting with existing ones, personalize your messages. Reference a shared interest, recent achievement, or a topic you both are passionate about. Personalized messages show that you value the relationship and are invested in the connection.

7.1.3 Offer Help and Support: Be proactive in offering help and support to your connections. Share relevant resources, introduce them to valuable contacts, or provide advice based on your expertise. By being helpful, you establish yourself as a trusted and valuable connection.

7.1.4 Networking Opportunities: Identify networking opportunities such as industry events, conferences, or LinkedIn Groups where you can connect with your connections in person or online. Actively participate in conversations and discussions, contribute value, and build stronger relationships.

7.2 Providing Value through Personalized Messaging and Engagement

To build trust and credibility on LinkedIn, it's crucial to provide value to your connections. Here are some strategies for providing value through personalized messaging and engagement:

7.2.1 Research and Relevance: Before reaching out to a connection, take the time to research their background, interests, and professional goals. This allows you to tailor your messages and engagement to their specific needs and interests.

7.2.2 Thoughtful Content Sharing: Share valuable and relevant content with your connections. This could be articles, blog posts, industry insights, or resources that you believe will be beneficial to them. Personalize your content recommendations based on their interests and areas of expertise.

7.2.3 Active Listening: Actively listen to your connections by paying attention to their updates, posts, and comments. Engage in meaningful conversations, offer insights, and provide support. Show that you value their opinions and perspectives.

7.2.4 Celebrate Successes: Recognize and celebrate the achievements and milestones of your connections. Congratulate them on promotions, new job opportunities, or professional accomplishments. This demonstrates your genuine interest and support for their success.

7.3 Using LinkedIn's Sales Navigator for Effective Relationship Management

LinkedIn's Sales Navigator is a powerful tool designed to enhance relationship management and lead generation. Here's how you can leverage Sales Navigator to nurture relationships effectively:

7.3.1 Advanced Search and Filtering: Utilize the advanced search and filtering capabilities of Sales Navigator to identify and target specific prospects or connections based on criteria such as industry, job title, location, or company size. This enables you to focus your efforts on the most relevant and valuable relationships.

7.3.2 Lead Recommendations: Sales Navigator provides lead recommendations based on your preferences and existing relationships. These lead recommendations can help you discover new prospects and expand your network. Take advantage of these recommendations to connect with potential clients or business partners.

7.3.3 Relationship Insights: Sales Navigator provides valuable insights about your connections, such as job changes, company updates, and shared connections. Stay informed about these insights to identify opportunities for engagement and conversation. Use this information to personalize your messages and provide relevant value to your connections.

7.3.4 InMail Messaging: With Sales Navigator, you have access to InMail, which allows you to send direct messages to LinkedIn members outside of your existing connections. This feature provides a valuable opportunity to reach out to prospects and start meaningful conversations. Craft personalized and compelling InMail messages to capture the attention of your target audience.

7.3.5 Account and Lead Management: Sales Navigator offers tools for managing your accounts and leads effectively. You can create lists to organize and prioritize your prospects, track interactions and engagements, and set reminders for follow-ups. These features help you stay organized and maintain a proactive approach to relationship management.

7.3.6 Team Collaboration: If you're working as part of a team, Sales Navigator provides collaborative features that enable you to share leads, notes, and insights with team members. This fosters effective communication and coordination, ensuring that everyone is aligned in their efforts to nurture relationships and drive business outcomes.

By leveraging LinkedIn's Sales Navigator, you can streamline your relationship management process, stay informed about valuable insights, and effectively engage with prospects and connections. It empowers you to take a more targeted and strategic approach to building trust and nurturing relationships on LinkedIn.

In conclusion, nurturing relationships and building trust are essential components of successful LinkedIn marketing. By focusing on building long-term relationships with your connections, providing value through personalized messaging and engagement, and utilizing tools like LinkedIn's Sales Navigator, you can establish yourself as a trusted professional, expand your network, and unlock new opportunities for growth and success. Remember, LinkedIn is not just a platform for self-promotion; it's a place to connect, engage, and build meaningful relationships that can propel your career or business forward.

Chapter 8

Measuring Success with LinkedIn Analytics

LinkedIn provides a robust set of analytics tools and insights that allow you to track the performance of your LinkedIn marketing efforts and make data-driven decisions. In this chapter, we will explore how to effectively utilize LinkedIn's analytics tools, track key performance metrics, and optimize your marketing strategy based on data and analytics.

8.1 Understanding LinkedIn Analytics

LinkedIn Analytics provides valuable insights into the performance of your LinkedIn profile, company page, and content. It offers a range of metrics and data points that can help you understand how your audience is engaging with your content, how your profile is performing, and how your company page is attracting followers and driving engagement.

To access LinkedIn Analytics, navigate to your LinkedIn profile or company page and click on the Analytics tab.

Here, you'll find a wealth of information to analyze and measure the success of your LinkedIn marketing efforts.

8.2 Key Metrics to Track on LinkedIn

8.2.1 Profile Metrics: LinkedIn Analytics provides data on profile views, connections, and search appearances. Monitoring these metrics can help you gauge the visibility and reach of your profile and identify opportunities to optimize it for better results.

8.2.2 Content Metrics: When it comes to content on LinkedIn, tracking metrics such as post views, likes, comments, and shares can provide insights into the performance and engagement of your posts. Additionally, LinkedIn offers data on follower demographics, allowing you to understand the composition of your audience and tailor your content accordingly.

8.2.3 Company Page Metrics: LinkedIn's analytics tools also provide data on your company page, including page views, follower growth, and engagement metrics. Monitoring these metrics can help you evaluate the effectiveness of your company page and make informed decisions to optimize its performance.

8.2.4 Conversion Metrics: LinkedIn offers conversion tracking capabilities that allow you to measure the effectiveness of your LinkedIn ad campaigns. By setting up conversion tracking, you can track actions such as website visits, form submissions, and downloads, providing valuable insights into the ROI of your advertising efforts.

8.3 Using LinkedIn Insights to Gain Actionable Data

LinkedIn Insights offers deeper analytics and demographic data on your audience, allowing you to gain actionable insights for your marketing strategy. Here are some key features of LinkedIn Insights:

8.3.1 Follower Insights: LinkedIn Insights provides information about your followers' job titles, locations, industries, and company sizes. This data helps you understand the composition of your audience and tailor your content to their preferences and needs.

8.3.2 Content Insights: With content insights, you can analyze the performance of your individual posts, track engagement metrics, and identify the types of content that resonate with your audience. This information can guide your content creation strategy and help you produce more engaging and relevant content.

8.3.3 Visitor Insights: LinkedIn Insights offers data on the visitors to your profile or company page. You can see who viewed your profile, their job titles, industries, and locations. This data can be useful for identifying potential leads or understanding the interest of your audience.

8.4 Optimizing Your Strategy Based on Data and Analytics

LinkedIn analytics provide you with the necessary data to optimize your marketing strategy and drive better results. Here are some tips to optimize your LinkedIn marketing strategy based on data and analytics:

8.4.1 Identify Top Performing Content: Analyze the performance of your content and identify the types of posts that receive the most engagement. Look for patterns and themes that resonate with your audience and incorporate them into your content strategy.

8.4.2 Tailor Your Content: Use the demographic data provided by LinkedIn Insights to tailor your content to the preferences and needs of your audience. Create content that addresses their pain points, provides value, and sparks engagement.

8.4.3 Test and Iterate: Use A/B testing to experiment with different types of content, headlines, and visuals. Analyze the results to understand what works best for your audience and refine your strategy accordingly.

8.4.4 Track Conversion Metrics: If you are running LinkedIn ad campaigns, track conversion metrics to evaluate the effectiveness of your ads. Optimize your campaigns based on the data to maximize your return on investment.

8.4.5 Monitor Competitors: LinkedIn Insights also allows you to gain insights into your competitors' performance. Monitor their activity, engagement metrics, and audience demographics to understand their strategies and identify areas for improvement in your own marketing efforts.

8.5 Reporting and Measurement

LinkedIn offers reporting features that allow you to export data and generate reports to track your progress and share insights with your team or stakeholders. Leverage these reporting capabilities to showcase the impact of your LinkedIn marketing efforts and make data-driven decisions.

In conclusion, LinkedIn's analytics tools and insights provide valuable data to measure the success of your LinkedIn marketing strategy. By tracking key performance metrics, utilizing LinkedIn Insights, and optimizing your strategy based on data and analytics, you can enhance your LinkedIn presence, engage your audience more effectively, and achieve your marketing goals on the platform. Remember, data-driven decision-making is crucial in harnessing the full potential of LinkedIn as a powerful marketing tool.

Chapter 9

LinkedIn Recruiting and Talent Acquisition

In today's competitive job market, companies need effective strategies to attract top talent and build a strong workforce. LinkedIn, with its extensive network of professionals and powerful recruitment features, has emerged as a go-to platform for talent acquisition. In this chapter, we will explore how to harness LinkedIn's power for talent acquisition, build a strong employer brand, and attract and hire top talent through the platform.

9.1 The Power of LinkedIn for Talent Acquisition

LinkedIn is a treasure trove of talent, with millions of professionals from various industries and backgrounds actively using the platform. Leveraging LinkedIn for talent acquisition offers numerous advantages:

- Extensive Professional Network: LinkedIn provides access to a vast pool of professionals, including passive job seekers who may not be actively searching for new opportunities but are open to considering them.

- Targeted Search Capabilities: LinkedIn's advanced search filters allow recruiters to narrow down their candidate search based on specific criteria, such as industry, location, job title, and skills, helping to find the most relevant candidates for their roles.

- Enhanced Candidate Insights: LinkedIn profiles provide detailed information about a candidate's professional background, experience, skills, recommendations, and endorsements. This information helps recruiters assess candidates' qualifications and suitability for the role.

9.2 Building a Strong Employer Brand on LinkedIn

A strong employer brand is crucial for attracting top talent and standing out in the competitive job market. LinkedIn offers several features and strategies to help build and showcase your employer brand effectively:

- Compelling Company Page: Optimize your LinkedIn company page to reflect your company's values, culture, and mission. Use engaging visuals, compelling descriptions, and employee testimonials to create a compelling and attractive employer brand.

- Employee Advocacy: Encourage your employees to actively engage on LinkedIn, share company updates, and provide insights into their roles and experiences. This employee advocacy can significantly enhance your employer brand and attract talent who resonate with your company culture.

- Thought Leadership: Establish yourself and your company as industry thought leaders by sharing valuable insights, expertise, and industry trends on LinkedIn. Publish articles, participate in relevant discussions, and engage with industry influencers to position your company as a knowledge leader.

9.3 Attracting and Hiring Top Talent through LinkedIn

LinkedIn offers several tools and features specifically designed to streamline the hiring process and attract top talent:

- Job Posts and Sponsored Jobs: Utilize LinkedIn's job posting and sponsored jobs features to showcase your open positions to a targeted audience. Craft compelling job descriptions, include relevant keywords, and utilize LinkedIn's targeting options to reach the right candidates.

- LinkedIn Recruiter: LinkedIn Recruiter is a powerful tool that allows recruiters to search and connect with potential candidates directly. It provides advanced search filters, messaging capabilities, and collaborative features to streamline the recruitment process.

- Employee Referrals: Leverage your employees' networks by implementing an employee referral program. Encourage your employees to refer qualified candidates, and offer incentives to reward successful referrals. Employee referrals often result in higher-quality candidates who are more likely to be a good fit for your organization.

9.4 Nurturing Candidate Relationships

Building strong relationships with candidates is crucial for successful talent acquisition. LinkedIn provides features and strategies to help recruiters nurture candidate relationships:

- Personalized Messaging: LinkedIn's messaging feature allows recruiters to engage with candidates directly and build personalized relationships. Use personalized messages to communicate with candidates, provide updates on their application status, and answer their questions promptly.

- Talent Pipelining: LinkedIn's talent pipelining feature enables recruiters to proactively build a pipeline of potential candidates for future positions. Engage with passive candidates, establish relationships, and keep them informed about your company's opportunities and updates.

- Candidate Relationship Management (CRM): LinkedIn offers CRM tools that enable recruiters to manage candidate relationships effectively. These tools allow recruiters to track interactions, set reminders, and stay organized throughout the recruitment process.

In conclusion, LinkedIn provides immense opportunities for talent acquisition and building a strong employer brand. By harnessing LinkedIn's power, optimizing your company page, showcasing your employer brand, utilizing recruitment tools, and nurturing candidate relationships, you can attract and hire top talent, gain a competitive edge in the job market, and build a strong and successful workforce. Embrace LinkedIn as a strategic platform for talent acquisition, and unlock its potential to transform your recruitment efforts.

Chapter 10

International and Global LinkedIn Marketing

In today's interconnected world, businesses are no longer confined to their local markets. With the rise of globalization, it has become increasingly important to develop a global marketing strategy that reaches audiences across different countries and cultures. LinkedIn, as a leading professional networking platform, offers powerful features and tools to help businesses expand their reach and engage with global audiences. In this chapter, we will explore the intricacies of international and global LinkedIn marketing and provide insights on how to adapt your strategy to overcome cultural and language barriers.

10.1 Expanding Your Reach with LinkedIn's International Features

LinkedIn offers a range of features that can significantly enhance your reach in international markets. By leveraging these features strategically, you can tap into new audiences and grow your global presence:

- Multilingual Profiles: LinkedIn allows users to create profiles in multiple languages. If you're targeting specific international markets, consider creating profiles in the local language to establish a stronger connection with local professionals.

- Location Targeting: LinkedIn's advertising platform enables you to target specific locations with your marketing campaigns. Utilize this feature to reach audiences in different countries and tailor your messaging accordingly.

- Global Network: LinkedIn's vast user base spans across the globe, providing access to professionals in various industries and countries. Expand your network by actively connecting with professionals from different regions, attending international events, and joining global LinkedIn groups.

10.2 Adapting Your Strategy for Global Audiences

While LinkedIn provides the tools to reach global audiences, it's essential to adapt your marketing strategy to resonate with these audiences. Consider the following strategies to effectively engage global LinkedIn users:

- Market Research: Conduct thorough market research to understand the cultural nuances, preferences, and trends of your target markets. This knowledge will help you tailor your content and messaging to align with the local audience's expectations.

- Localized Content: Adapt your content to suit the local language and cultural context. Translating your content is a good starting point, but it's also important to ensure that your messaging is culturally relevant and resonates with the target audience.

- Local Influencers and Partnerships: Collaborate with local influencers and industry experts to amplify your reach and establish credibility in new markets. Partnering with local businesses or organizations can also help you gain a foothold in international markets.

- Global Events and Webinars: Participate in global industry events and webinars to showcase your expertise and connect with professionals from different countries.

These platforms provide opportunities to network, share knowledge, and build relationships with a global audience.

10.3 Overcoming Cultural and Language Barriers on LinkedIn

When expanding internationally, it's crucial to be aware of cultural and language barriers that may impact your marketing efforts on LinkedIn. Consider the following strategies to overcome these challenges:

- Cultural Sensitivity: Gain an understanding of the cultural norms, values, and sensitivities of your target markets. Avoid cultural faux pas and ensure that your content and messaging align with the cultural expectations of each market.

- Language Localization: Beyond translating your content, consider localizing it to reflect the language nuances and preferences of the target market. This may include adapting idioms, using appropriate terminology, and tailoring your messaging to local customs.

- Engaging Local Professionals: Collaborate with local professionals or hire local talent who have a deep understanding of the local culture and language. They can provide valuable insights and ensure that your marketing efforts are culturally appropriate and resonate with the target audience.

- Cross-Cultural Communication: LinkedIn provides opportunities to connect with professionals from different cultural backgrounds. Be mindful of cross-cultural communication norms, such as greetings, business etiquette, and communication styles, to build meaningful relationships with professionals from diverse cultures.

In conclusion, expanding your LinkedIn marketing efforts internationally requires a thoughtful and adaptable approach. By leveraging LinkedIn's international features, adapting your strategy to suit global

audiences, and overcoming cultural and language barriers, you can unlock new opportunities, connect with professionals worldwide, and establish a strong global presence. Embrace the power of international LinkedIn marketing and position your business for success in the global marketplace.

Chapter 11

Future Trends in LinkedIn Marketing

LinkedIn is a dynamic platform that continuously evolves to meet the changing needs and preferences of its users. As a savvy marketer, it's crucial to stay updated on the latest trends and emerging features on LinkedIn to maintain a competitive edge. In this chapter, we will explore the future trends in LinkedIn marketing and discuss strategies to adapt and thrive in the ever-changing landscape of professional networking.

11.1 Exploring Emerging Features and Opportunities on LinkedIn

LinkedIn consistently introduces new features and tools to enhance the user experience and provide additional marketing opportunities. By keeping an eye on these emerging features, you can leverage them to maximize your LinkedIn marketing efforts. Here are some emerging trends and features to watch out for:

- LinkedIn Live: LinkedIn Live is a live streaming feature that allows you to broadcast real-time videos to your network. Embrace this engaging format to connect with your audience, share valuable insights, and host interactive events.

- LinkedIn Stories: Similar to other social media platforms, LinkedIn has introduced Stories, which are short-lived, vertical content that appears at the top of the user's feed. Utilize this feature to showcase behind-the-scenes moments, share quick tips, and humanize your brand.

- LinkedIn Events: LinkedIn Events provide a platform for hosting virtual or in-person events, such as webinars, conferences, or workshops. Take advantage of this feature to promote your events, generate registrations, and engage with attendees.

- LinkedIn Polls: Polls are an interactive way to gather insights and engage your audience. Create polls on LinkedIn to solicit opinions, gather feedback, and encourage participation from your network.

- LinkedIn Creator Mode: Creator Mode is a feature that highlights your content and enhances your personal brand on LinkedIn. It enables you to showcase your expertise, increase visibility, and attract relevant connections.

11.2 Adapting to Evolving User Behaviors and Platform Changes

As LinkedIn evolves, so do the behaviors and expectations of its users. To stay relevant and effectively engage your audience, it's crucial to understand and adapt to these evolving user behaviors. Here are some key considerations:

- Mobile Optimization: With the increasing use of mobile devices, ensure that your LinkedIn content and profile are optimized for mobile viewing. Use mobile-friendly visuals, concise captions, and easily readable formats to cater to users on the go.

- Video Content Dominance: Video content continues to dominate social media platforms, and LinkedIn is no exception. Embrace video marketing on LinkedIn to capture attention, deliver your message effectively, and showcase your expertise.

- Authenticity and Transparency: LinkedIn users value authenticity and transparency. Share authentic stories, highlight your company culture, and provide genuine insights to build trust and credibility with your audience.

- Personalized Engagement: Personalization is becoming increasingly important on LinkedIn. Tailor your messages and content to individual connections, address their specific needs, and foster personalized conversations to build stronger relationships.

- LinkedIn as a Learning Platform: LinkedIn Learning has gained popularity as a platform for professional development. Consider creating educational content, sharing industry insights, and positioning yourself as a thought leader in your field.

11.3 Staying Ahead in the Dynamic World of LinkedIn Marketing

To excel in LinkedIn marketing, you must be proactive and adaptable. Here are some strategies to stay ahead of the curve:

- Continuous Learning: Stay updated on the latest LinkedIn features, trends, and best practices through industry publications, LinkedIn resources, and networking with fellow professionals. Attend webinars, conferences, and workshops to expand your knowledge and skills.

- A/B Testing and Experimentation: Test different strategies, content formats, and messaging on LinkedIn to understand what resonates best with your audience. Experimentation allows you to optimize your approach and adapt to changing user preferences.

- Data-Driven Decision Making: Leverage LinkedIn analytics and data to gain insights into your performance, audience engagement, and content effectiveness. Analyze the data to inform your strategy, make data-driven decisions, and identify areas for improvement.

- Networking and Collaboration: LinkedIn is a powerful networking platform. Actively engage with your connections, participate in relevant LinkedIn groups, and collaborate with other professionals in your industry. Networking can lead to valuable partnerships, collaborations, and business opportunities.

- Adaptability and Agility: LinkedIn is constantly evolving, and it's essential to be adaptable and agile in your marketing approach. Embrace change, experiment with new features, and adjust your strategy to align with the evolving trends and user behaviors.

By staying informed about emerging features, adapting to evolving user behaviors, and embracing a proactive mindset, you can position yourself as a LinkedIn marketing expert and leverage the platform's full potential for your business's success.

LinkedIn marketing offers immense opportunities for professionals and businesses to connect, engage, and grow. By optimizing your profile, building a strong network, creating compelling content, leveraging LinkedIn's features, and staying ahead of future trends, you can harness the full potential of LinkedIn to achieve your marketing goals and propel your career or business forward. The strategies and insights shared in this book will serve as your roadmap to mastering LinkedIn marketing and achieving remarkable results. Embrace the power of LinkedIn and unlock a world of possibilities for your professional and business growth.

Appendix

Tools for LinkedIn Marketing

In addition to the strategies and techniques discussed in this book, there are several useful tools and resources available that can further enhance your LinkedIn marketing efforts. These tools can help streamline your workflow, improve productivity, and provide valuable insights to optimize your LinkedIn strategy. In this appendix, we will explore some of the top tools for LinkedIn marketing.

1. LinkedIn Sales Navigator: LinkedIn Sales Navigator is a powerful tool designed for sales professionals and teams. It provides advanced search and lead generation capabilities, allowing you to find and connect with potential clients and customers. Sales Navigator also offers features such as lead recommendations, account and lead management, and real-time sales updates, helping you build relationships and close deals more effectively.

2. Hootsuite: Hootsuite is a popular social media management platform that supports LinkedIn along with other social media networks. With Hootsuite, you can

schedule and publish LinkedIn posts, monitor engagement, track keywords and hashtags, and manage multiple LinkedIn accounts in one place. It provides analytics and reporting features to measure the performance of your LinkedIn campaigns and gather insights for optimization.

3. Buffer: Buffer is another social media management tool that supports LinkedIn. It allows you to schedule and publish posts, analyze engagement metrics, and manage multiple LinkedIn profiles. Buffer offers a user-friendly interface and provides valuable data and analytics to help you make informed decisions about your LinkedIn content strategy.

4. Canva: Canva is a versatile graphic design tool that offers a wide range of templates and design elements to create visually appealing content for LinkedIn. With Canva, you can design professional-looking images, infographics, presentations, and more. It also provides pre-sized templates for LinkedIn posts and cover images, making it easy to create visually engaging content that aligns with LinkedIn's design guidelines.

5. LinkedIn Elevate: LinkedIn Elevate is a tool designed to facilitate employee advocacy and content sharing. It

allows companies to curate and share content with their employees, who can then share it with their LinkedIn networks. Elevate helps amplify your brand's reach, enhance employee engagement, and increase the visibility of your content on LinkedIn.

6. Crystal: Crystal is an AI-powered tool that provides personality insights based on LinkedIn profiles. It analyzes the language and behavior patterns of individuals and offers guidance on how to effectively communicate with them. Crystal can help you tailor your messaging and approach when connecting with potential clients, partners, or employees on LinkedIn.

7. Google Analytics: Although not specific to LinkedIn, Google Analytics is a valuable tool for tracking website traffic and understanding the impact of your LinkedIn marketing efforts on your website. By integrating Google Analytics with your LinkedIn campaigns, you can gain insights into the performance of LinkedIn-generated traffic, track conversions, and measure the ROI of your LinkedIn marketing activities.

8. LinkedIn Pulse: LinkedIn Pulse is a publishing platform within LinkedIn that allows you to share long-form

articles and blog posts with your LinkedIn network. It provides an opportunity to showcase your expertise, establish thought leadership, and engage with a wider audience on LinkedIn. Publishing articles on LinkedIn Pulse can help boost your visibility and credibility within your industry.

9. LinkedIn Learning: LinkedIn Learning (formerly Lynda.com) is an online learning platform that offers a wide range of courses on various topics, including marketing, sales, and professional development. Utilizing LinkedIn Learning can help you stay updated with the latest industry trends, acquire new skills, and further enhance your LinkedIn marketing knowledge.

10. LinkedIn Analytics: LinkedIn provides its own analytics and insights tool, which offers data on profile views, engagement, and audience demographics. It can help you measure the performance of your LinkedIn profile, content, and campaigns. LinkedIn Analytics provides valuable information to refine your strategy, understand your audience, and optimize your LinkedIn marketing efforts.

These are just a few examples of the many tools available to support

your LinkedIn marketing activities. Each tool serves a specific purpose and offers unique features to enhance your LinkedIn presence and drive better results. Depending on your specific needs and goals, you can explore and experiment with different tools to find the ones that best suit your requirements.

Remember, while tools can be helpful, it's essential to align them with your overall LinkedIn marketing strategy and use them strategically. Regularly evaluate the effectiveness of the tools you employ and make adjustments as necessary to optimize your LinkedIn marketing efforts.

By leveraging the power of these tools, you can streamline your workflow, improve productivity, and gain valuable insights to elevate your LinkedIn marketing game. Take advantage of these resources and stay up-to-date with new tools and technologies that emerge in the dynamic world of LinkedIn marketing.

Conclusion

Unleashing the Full Potential of LinkedIn for Your Business or Professional Career

Congratulations! By completing this comprehensive guide on mastering LinkedIn marketing, you have equipped yourself with the knowledge, strategies, and tools to unlock the full potential of LinkedIn for your business or professional career. You are now ready to take your LinkedIn presence to new heights and achieve remarkable results.

Throughout this book, we have explored the power of LinkedIn as a marketing platform and discussed various aspects of leveraging its features to your advantage. From optimizing your profile to building a strong network, creating compelling content, utilizing LinkedIn's advertising capabilities, and staying ahead of future trends, you have gained a deep understanding of how to maximize your impact on this professional networking platform.

By implementing the strategies outlined in this guide, you can establish yourself as a thought leader, attract new connections and customers, nurture valuable relationships, and ultimately achieve your marketing goals on LinkedIn. Whether you are a business owner, a marketer, a job seeker, or a professional looking to expand your network, LinkedIn offers a wealth of opportunities to showcase your expertise, grow your brand, and advance your career.

As you embark on your LinkedIn marketing journey, keep in mind the following key takeaways:

1. Your LinkedIn Profile is Your Digital Business Card: Craft a compelling and professional LinkedIn profile that highlights your expertise, achievements, and unique value proposition. Optimize it for search and make a strong first impression on visitors.

2. Building a Network is Essential: Expand your LinkedIn network strategically by connecting with industry professionals, colleagues, clients, and potential partners. Foster meaningful relationships by engaging with your connections and providing value through thoughtful interactions.

3. Content is King: Create and share high-quality, engaging content that resonates with your target audience. Whether it's articles, posts, videos, or curated content, aim to provide value, spark conversations, and position yourself as a trusted authority in your field.

4. LinkedIn Advertising: Explore the various advertising options LinkedIn offers, such as sponsored content, lead generation forms, and LinkedIn ads. Leverage these tools to reach a wider audience, generate leads, and drive meaningful conversions.

5. Stay Ahead of Trends: LinkedIn is a dynamic platform, and staying informed about emerging features, user behaviors, and industry trends is crucial. Continuously learn, adapt, and experiment to remain at the forefront of LinkedIn marketing.

Remember, success on LinkedIn requires consistency, authenticity, and an ongoing commitment to building relationships and delivering value. It's a long-term investment that yields substantial rewards when approached with the right strategies and a genuine desire to connect and engage.

As you continue your LinkedIn marketing journey, keep exploring new ways to optimize your presence, refine your strategies, and adapt to the evolving landscape. Monitor your performance, analyze data, and make data-driven decisions to continually improve and achieve even greater success.

Lastly, remember that mastering LinkedIn marketing is a continuous process. As the platform evolves and new opportunities arise, stay curious, open-minded, and willing to embrace change. Keep expanding your knowledge, networking with industry peers, and staying informed about the latest updates to ensure you remain at the forefront of LinkedIn marketing.

Congratulations once again on becoming a LinkedIn marketing master! Embrace the power of LinkedIn, unleash its full potential, and enjoy the growth and success that it brings to your business or professional career. Good luck!

www.ingramcontent.com/pod-product-compliance
Lightning Source LLC
Chambersburg PA
CBHW050250220526
45465CB00002B/628